A
DIFFERENT SKY

A DIFFERENT SKY

A Poetry Anthology for GCSE   Peter Ellison

Edward Arnold

A division of Hodder & Stoughton

LONDON   MELBOURNE   AUCKLAND

© 1988 Peter Ellison

First published in Great Britain 1988

British Library Cataloguing in Publication Data

   A Different sky : a poetry anthology for GCSE
   1. Poetry in English — Anthologies — for schools
   I. Ellison, Peter
   821′.008

   ISBN 0–7131–7812–4

Typeset by Gecko Ltd, Bicester, Oxon
Printed in Great Britain for Edward Arnold, the educational, academic and
medical publishing division of Hodder and Stoughton Ltd, Mill Road, Dunton
Green, Sevenoaks, Kent by St Edmundsbury Press, Bury St Edmunds, Suffolk

Contents

Acknowledgments

The publishers would like to thank the following for their kind permission to reproduce poems in this volume:

Faber & Faber Ltd for 'What I Expected' from *Collected Poems* by Stephen Spender, 'Digging for China' from *Poems 1943–1956* by Richard Wilbur, 'On Roofs of Terry Street' from *Terry Street* by Douglas Dunn, 'Scaffolding' from *Death of a Naturalist* by Seamus Heaney, 'Stop all the clocks, cut off the telephone' from *Collected Poems* by W.H. Auden, 'The Locust' from *The Rattle Bag*; Robert Morgan for '4C Boy' © Robert Morgan 1967 from *Welsh Voices* published by J.M. Dent and Sons Ltd; Michael Hamburger/Carcanet Press, Manchester for 'Paddington Canal' from *Collected Poems*, 1984, 1985 by Michael Hamburger; New Directions Publishing Corp., New York for 'Philomena Andronico' from *Collected Later Poems* © 1948 by William Carlos Williams; Richard Kell/Chatto & Windus for 'Fishing Harbour Towards Evening' from *Control Tower* by Richard Kell; Fred D'Aguiar/Chatto & Windus for 'The Day Mama Dot Takes Ill' from *Mama Dot* by Fred D'Aguiar; W.H. Allen for 'Tonight at Noon' from *Tonight at Noon* by Adrian Henri; Oxford University Press for 'A Martian Sends a Postcard Home' from *A Martian Sends a Postcard Home* by Craig Raine (1979), 'The Telephone Call' and 'Witnesses' from *The Incident Book* by Fleur Adcock (1986), 'The Marriage' from Anne Stevenson's *Selected Poems 1956–1986* (1987); George MacBeth for 'Scissor-Man' from George MacBeth's *Collected Poems* published by Macmillan; Harcourt Brace Jovanovich, Inc., Orlando, Florida for 'Worms and the Wind' from *The Complete Poems of Carl Sandburg*, copyright 1950 by Carl Sandburg, renewed 1978 by Margaret Sandburg, Helga Sandburg Crile and Janet Sandburg; Penguin Books Ltd for 'In the Microscope' and 'The Lesson' from *Selected Poems of Miroslav Holub* translated by Ian Milner and George Theiner (Penguin Modern European Poets, 1967), copyright © Miroslav Holub, 1967, translation copyright © Penguin Books, 1967; André Deutsch Ltd for 'In Nature' from *The Stone Harp* by John Haines; Jonathan Cape Ltd for 'a cat, a horse and the sun' from *After the Merrymaking* by Roger McGough; Century Hutchinson Publishing Group Ltd for 'Life-Style' from *The Complete Little Ones* by Gavin Ewart, 'Last Chance, Last Hope' from *The Region's Violence* by Ruth Fainlight both published by Hutchinson; David Holbrook for 'Fingers in the Door' from *Imaginings* by David Holbrook published by The Bodley Head; David Higham Associates Ltd for 'Early Morning Feed' from *The Collector* by Peter Redgrove published by Routledge and Kegan Paul; Olwyn Hughes for 'Morning Song' from *Collected Poems* by Sylvia Plath published by Faber & Faber Ltd, London, copyright Ted Hughes 1965 and 1981; David Higham Associates Ltd for 'Bear-Hug', 'Miss Butterfly, Miss Moth', 'Masks', 'Chrysalis' and 'The Lion from Rio' from *The Lion from Rio* by Penelope Shuttle published by Oxford University Press; Martin Secker & Warburg Ltd for 'Meeting, 1944' from *The Photographer in Winter* by George Szirtes; The Blackstaff Press, Belfast for 'Nessa' from *The Selected Paul Durcan*; David Higham Associates Ltd for 'New Face' from *Revolutionary Petunias and Other Poems* by Alice Walker published by The Women's Press; Polygon for 'Rapunzstiltskin' from *Dreaming Frankenstein and Collected Poems* by Liz Lochhead; Virago Press for 'Friend' from *Kisses for Mayakovsky* by Alison Fell, 'Small Questions Asked by the Fat Black Woman' from *The Fat Black Woman's Poems* by Grace Nichols, 'Still I Rise' from *And Still I Rise* by Maya Angelou; Rosemary Norman for 'Waterloo Station' from *Dancing the Tightrope* by Rosemary Norman published by The Women's Press; Unwin Hyman for 'The Projectionist's Nightmare' from *Notes to the Hurrying Man* by Brian Patten; Jonathan Cape Ltd/Henry Holt & Company Inc., New York for 'On a Tree Fallen Across the Road' copyright 1923 and renewed 1951 by Robert Frost from *The Poetry of Robert Frost* edited by Edward Connery Lathem; Grafton Books (a division of the Collins Publishing Group) for 'Lore' from *Selected Poems 1946–1968* by R.S. Thomas; Dolmen Press Ltd for 'Heirloom' from *The Lost Country* by Kathleen Raine; Alfred A. Knopf Inc. for 'I, too, sing America' copyright by Alfred A. Knopf Inc. 1926 and renewed 1954 by Langston Hughes from *Selected Poems of Langston Hughes*; Broadside Press, Detroit for 'Right on: white america' from *We a baddDD people* by Sonia Sanchez; Brian Meeks for his poem 'Las' Rights' from *The Penguin Book of Caribbean Verse in English*, 1986; Bogle-L'Ouverture Publications Ltd for 'Yuh Hear Bout?' by Valerie Bloom from *News from Babylon*, ed. J. Berry published by Chatto & Windus; Pamela Mordecai for her poem 'Tell Me' from *The Penguin Book of Caribbean Verse in English*, 1986.

Every effort has been made to trace and acknowledge ownership of copyright. The publishers will be glad to make suitable arrangements with copyright holders of the following whom it has not been possible to contact:

'Stillbirth' by Barbara Noel Scott
'Evolution' by Edwin Brock
'Witch' by Jean Tepperman

The publishers would also like to thank the following for permission to reproduce photographs in this book: Barnaby's Picture Library (p.1); Sally and Richard Greenhill (pp.25 and 35); Barbara Kruger (p. 49); Format Photographers Ltd/Maggie Murray (p. 59); Vision International (p.11).

To the Teacher

A Different Sky is a teaching anthology of contemporary poetry designed for use with GCSE and Standard Grade English and English Literature classes. It comprises six units, each of which can be taught independently.

To gain the most from the arrangement of the poems, students will need the accompanying *Resource Book* which provides activities on each poem. These activities are presented on photocopiable worksheets and are designed to enable discussion and comparison. A wide variety of written assignments is also included. Most of the worksheets involve the manipulation of the text by students (DARTs–based activities) and can be used independently of the rest of the unit. They provide the impetus for the kind of lively discussion that powerful poetry deserves.

UNIT
1

A Different Sky

What I Expected

What I expected was
Thunder, fighting,
Long struggles with men
And climbing.
After continual straining
I should grow strong;
Then the rocks would shake,
And I rest long.

What I had not foreseen
Was the gradual day
Weakening the will
Leaking the brightness away,
The lack of good to touch,
The fading of body and soul
—Smoke before wind,
Corrupt, unsubstantial.

The wearing of Time,
And the watching of cripples pass
With limbs shaped like questions
In their odd twist,
The pulverous grief
Melting the bones with pity,
The sick falling from earth—
These, I could not foresee.

Expecting always
Some brightness to hold in trust,
Some final innocence
Exempt from dust,
That, hanging solid,
Would dangle through all,
Like the created poem,
Or faceted crystal.

STEPHEN SPENDER

Digging for China

'Far enough down is China,' somebody said.
'Dig deep enough and you might see the sky
As clear as at the bottom of a well.
Except it would be real – a different sky.
Then you could burrow down until you came
To China! Oh, it's nothing like New Jersey.
There's people, trees, and houses, and all that,
But much, much different. Nothing looks the same.'

I went and got the trowel out of the shed
And sweated like a coolie all that morning,
Digging a hole beside the lilac-bush,
Down on my hands and knees. It was a sort
Of praying, I suspect. I watched my hand
Dig deep and darker, and I tried and tried
To dream a place where nothing was the same.
The trowel never did break through to blue.

Before the dream could weary of itself
My eyes were tired of looking into darkness,
My sunbaked head of hanging down a hole.
I stood up in a place I had forgotten,
Blinking and staggering while the earth went round
And showed me silver barns, the fields dozing
In palls of brightness, patens* growing and gone
In the tides of leaves, and the whole sky china blue.
Until I got my balance back again
All that I saw was China, China, China.

RICHARD WILBUR

*dishes *or* plates

4C Boy

He was passive, one of seven,
With a subnormal gait and a confused
Brain damaged by the evils of home
And the mean cells of heredity.
His speech was slow, peculiar,
Asthmatic, his face flushed
With fear imposed by classmates
In quiet corners of playgrounds.
His bitten fingers moved
With spastic slowness, his glasses
Pressed against his eyebrows
And his fleshy ears stuck out
Like two discs of pink plasticine.
Words on paper were strange
Symbols for his dull eyes
And ripped thoughts. Painting
Was his only source of joy.
When he laboured on rich compositions
His eyes glared over hoghaired
Brush and sugar paper.
His work sparkled with colour;
Fantasies from his imagination forced
Black unending lines of tension
Around shimmering abstract shapes.
His paintings reminded me of a tropical
Garden full of rainbows and birds
Where the sun shone in lemon yellow
Over a stream flowing with tears of despair.

ROBERT MORGAN

Paddington Canal

A mocking mirror, the black water turns
Tall houses upside down, makes learned men
Walk on their heads in squares of burning light:
Lovers like folded bats hang in a kiss
Swaying as if a breeze could severe them.
The barges, giant sea-birds fast asleep,
Lie on the surface, moored and motionless;
Then, drowning gently, are drawn down to join
The sunken lovers and the acrobats.

Out of the grim dimensions of a street
Slowly I see another landscape grow
Downwards into a lost reality;
A magic mirror, the black water tells
Of a reversed Atlantis wisely built
To catch and to transform
The wasted substance of our daily acts,
Accommodate our mad and lovely doubles
In a more graceful city timelessly.

MICHAEL HAMBURGER

On Roofs of Terry Street

Television aerials, Chinese characters
In the lower sky, wave gently in the smoke.

Nest-building sparrows peck at moss,
Urban flora and fauna, soft, unscrupulous.

Rain drying on the slates shines sometimes.
A builder is repairing someone's leaking roof.

He kneels upright to rest his back.
His trowel catches the light and becomes precious.

DOUGLAS DUNN

Philomena Andronico

With the boys busy
at ball
in the worn lot
nearby

She stands in
the short street
reflectively bouncing
the red ball

Slowly
practiced
a little awkwardly
throwing one leg over

(Not as she had done
formerly
screaming and
missing

But slowly
surely) then
pausing throws
the ball

With a full slow
very slow
and easy motion
following through

With a slow
half turn—
as the ball flies
and rolls gently

At the child's feet
waiting—
and yet he misses
it and turns

And runs while she
slowly
regains her former
pose

Then shoves her fingers
up through
her loose short hair
quickly

Draws one stocking
tight and
waiting
tilts

Her hips and
in the warm still
air lets
her arms
        Fall

Fall
loosely
(waiting)
at her sides

WILLIAM CARLOS WILLIAMS

Fishing Harbour Towards Evening

Slashed clouds leak gold. Along the slurping wharf
The snugged boats creak and seesaw. Round the masts

Abrasive squalls flake seagulls off the sky:
Choppy with wings the rapids of shrill sound.

Wrapt in spliced airs of fish and tar,
Light wincing on their knives, the clockwork men

Incise and scoop the oily pouches, flip
The soft guts overboard with blood-wet fingers.

Among three rhythms the slapping silver turns
To polished icy marble upon the deck.

RICHARD KELL

The Locust

What is a locust?
Its head, a grain of corn; its neck, the hinge of a knife;
Its horns, a bit of thread; its chest is smooth and
    burnished;
Its body is like a knife-handle;
Its hock, a saw; its spittle, ink;
Its underwings, clothing for the dead.
On the ground—it is laying eggs;
In flight—it is like the clouds.
Approaching the ground, it is rain glittering in the sun;
Lighting on a plant, it becomes a pair of scissors;
Walking, it becomes a razor;
Desolation walks with it.

ANON

From the Malagasy (trans. A. Marre and Willard R. Trask)

UNIT
2

The Martian Postcard

Tonight at Noon*

(for Charles Mingus and Clayton Squares)

Tonight at noon
Supermarkets will advertise 3d *EXTRA* on everything
Tonight at noon
Children from happy families will be sent to live in a home
Elephants will tell each other human jokes
America will declare peace on Russia
World War I generals will sell poppies in the streets on
        November 11th
The first daffodils of autumn will appear
When the leaves fall upwards to the trees

Tonight at noon
Pigeons will hunt cats through city backyards
Hitler will tell us to fight on the beaches and on the
        landing fields
A tunnel full of water will be built under Liverpool
Pigs will be sighted flying in formation over Woolton
and Nelson will not only get his eye back but his arm as
        well
White Americans will demonstrate for equal rights
in front of the Black House
and the Monster has just created Dr Frankenstein

Girls in bikinis are moonbathing
Folksongs are being sung by real folk
Artgalleries are closed to people over 21
Poets get their poems in the Top 20
Politicians are elected to insane asylums
There's jobs for everyone and nobody wants them
In back alleys everywhere teenage lovers are kissing
in broad daylight

In forgotten graveyards everywhere the dead will quietly
bury the living
and
You will tell me you love me
Tonight at noon

*The title for this poem is taken from an LP by Charles
Mingus 'Tonight at Noon', Atlantic 1416.

ADRIAN HENRI

A Martian Sends a Postcard Home

Caxtons are mechanical birds with many wings
and some are treasured for their markings–

they cause the eyes to melt
or the body to shriek without pain.

I have never seen one fly, but
sometimes they perch on the hand.

Mist is when the sky is tired of flight
and rests its soft machine on ground:

then the world is dim and bookish
like engravings under tissue paper

Rain is when the earth is television.
It has the property of making colours darker.

Model T is a room with the lock inside –
a key is turned to free the world

for movement, so quick there is a film
to watch for anything missed.

But time is tied to the wrist
or kept in a box, ticking with impatience.

In homes, a haunted apparatus sleeps,
that snores when you pick it up.

If the ghost cries, they carry it
to their lips and soothe it to sleep

with sounds. And yet, they wake it up
deliberately, by tickling with a finger.

Only the young are allowed to suffer
openly. Adults go to a punishment room

with water but nothing to eat.
They lock the door and suffer the noises

alone. No one is exempt
and everyone's pain has a different smell.

At night, when all the colours die,
they hide in pairs

and read about themselves–
in colour, with their eyelids shut.

CRAIG RAINE

Scissor-Man

I am dangerous
   in a crisis
with sharp legs and a screw

   in my genitals. I slice
bacon-rind for a living. At nights I
   lie dried

under the draining-board, dreaming
   of Nutcrackers
and the Carrot-grater. If I should

   catch him rubbing
those tin nipples of hers
   in the bread-bin

(God rust his pivot!) so much for
   secrecy. I'd have his
washer off. And

   then what? It scarcely pays
to be 'Made In Hamburg'. Even
   our little salt-spoon

can sound snooty
   with an E.P.N.S. under
his armpit. Even the pie-server

   who needs re-dipping. In sixteen
stainless years dividing
   chippolata-links I

am still denied
   a place in the sink unit. And
you can imagine

   what pairing-off is possible
with a wriggle of cork-screws
   in an open knife-box. So I

keep my legs
   crossed. I never cut up
rough. I lie with care

in a world where a squint leg
could be fatal. I sleep like a weapon
with a yen for a pierced ear.

GEORGE MACBETH

The Telephone Call

They asked me 'Are you sitting down?
Right? This is Universal Lotteries',
they said. 'You've won the top prize,
the Ultra-super Global Special.
What would you do with a million pounds?
Or, actually, with more than a million–
not that it makes a lot of difference
once you're a millionaire.' And they laughed.

'Are you OK?' they asked–'Still there?
Come on, now, tell us, how does it feel?'
I said 'I just . . . I can't believe it!'
They said 'That's what they all say.
What else? Go on, tell us about it.'
I said 'I feel the top of my head
has floated off, out through the window,
revolving like a flying saucer.'

'That's unusual' they said. 'Go on.'
I said 'I'm finding it hard to talk.
My throat's gone dry, my nose is tingling.
I think I'm going to sneeze–or cry.'
'That's right' they said, 'don't be ashamed
of giving way to your emotions.
It isn't every day you hear
you're going to get a million pounds.

Relax, now, have a little cry;
we'll give you a moment. . . ' 'Hang on!' I said.
'I haven't bought a lottery ticket
for years and years. And what did you say
the company's called?' They laughed again.
'Not to worry about a ticket.
We're Universal. We operate
a Retrospective Chances Module.

Nearly everyone's bought a ticket
in some lottery or another,
once at least. We buy up the files,
feed the names into our computer,

and see who the lucky person is.'
'Well, that's incredible' I said.
'It's marvellous. I still can't quite . . .
I'll believe it when I see the cheque.'

'Oh,' they said, 'there's no cheque.'
'But the money?''We don't deal in money.
Experiences are what we deal in.
You've had a great experience, right?
Exciting? Something you'll remember?
That's your prize. So congratulations
from all of us at Universal.
Have a nice day!' And the line went dead.

FLEUR ADCOCK

Worms and the Wind

Worms would rather be worms.
Ask a worm and he says, 'Who knows what a worm
    knows?'
Worms go down and up and over and under.
Worms like tunnels.
When worms talk they talk about the worm world.
Worms like it in the dark.
Neither the sun nor the moon interests a worm.
Zigzag worms hate circle worms.
Curve worms never trust square worms.
Worms know what worms want.
Slide worms are suspicious of crawl worms.
One worm asks another, 'How does your belly drag today?'
The shape of a crooked worm satisfies a crooked worm.
A straight worm says, 'Why not be straight?'
Worms tired of crawling begin to slither.
Long worms slither farther than short worms.
Middle-sized worms say, 'It is nice to be neither long nor short.'
Old worms teach young worms to say, 'Don't be sorry for
    me unless you
have been a worm and lived in worm places and read
    worm books.'
When worms go to war they dig in, come out and fight,
    dig in again,
come out and fight again, dig in again, and so on.
Worms underground never hear the wind overground
    and sometimes they
ask, 'What is this wind we hear of?'

CARL SANDBURG

In the Microscope

Here too are dreaming landscapes,
lunar, derelict.
Here too are the masses
tillers of the soil.
And cells, fighters
who lay down their lives
for a song.

Here too are cemeteries,
fame and snow.
And I hear murmuring,
the revolt of immense estates.

MIROSLAV HOLUB

(trans. I.Milner and G.Theiner)

In Nature

Here too are life's victims,
captives of an old umbrella,
lives wrecked
by the lifting of a stone.

Sailors marooned
on the island of a leaf
when their ship
of mud and straw went down.

Explorers lost
among roots and raindrops,
drunkards sleeping it off
in the fields of pollen.

Cities of sand that fall,
dust towers that blow away.
Penal colonies
from which no one returns.

Here too, neighbourhoods
in revolt, revengeful columns;
evenings at the broken wall,
black armies in flight . . .

JOHN HAINES

a cat, a horse and the sun

a cat mistrusts the sun
keeps out of its way
only where sun and shadow meet
it moves

a horse loves the sun
it basks all day
snorts
and beats its hooves

the sun likes horses
but hates cats
that is why it makes hay
and heats tin roofs

ROGER MCGOUGH

Life-Style

The farmyard squeals in the breakfast bacon

The sun is shining in the noble vintage

The eggs are clucking in the honourable omelette

The wheat is windswept in the loaves we love so

In the beefburgers the bulls are bellowing

The peat-clean water wobbles through the whisky

The calmness of cows murmurs in the milk

GAVIN EWART

UNIT
3

Parents and Children

Fingers in the Door

Careless for an instant I closed my child's fingers in the jamb. She
Held her breath, contorted the whole of her being, foetus-wise,
   against the
Burning fact of the pain. And for a moment
I wished myself dispersed in a hundred thousand pieces
Among the dead bright stars. The child's cry broke,
She clung to me, and it crowded in to me how she and I were
Light-years from any mutual help or comfort. For her I cast seed
Into her mother's womb; cells grew and launched itself as a being:
Nothing restores her to my being, or ours, even to the mother who
   within her
Carried and quickened, bore, and sobbed at her separation, despite
   all my envy,
Nothing can restore. She, I, mother, sister, dwell dispersed among
   dead bright stars:
We are there in our hundred thousand pieces!

DAVID HOLBROOK

Early Morning Feed

The father darts out on the stairs
To listen to that keening
In the upper room, for a change of note
That signifies distress, to scotch disaster,
The kettle humming in the room behind.

He thinks, on tiptoe, ears a-strain,
The cool dawn rising like the moon:
'Must not appear and pick him up;
He mustn't think he has me springing
To his beck and call,'
The kettle rattling behind the kitchen door.

He has him springing
A-quiver on the landing –
For a distress-note, a change of key,
To gallop up the stairs to him
To take him up, light as a violin,
And stroke his back until he smiles.
He sidles in the kitchen
And pours his tea . . .

And again stands hearkening
For milk cracking the lungs.
There's a little panting,
A cough: the thumb's in: he'll sleep,
The cup of tea cooling on the kitchen table.

Can he go in now to his chair and think
Of the miracle of breath, pick up a book,
Ready at all times to take it at a run
And intervene between him and disaster,
Sipping his cold tea as the sun comes up?

He returns to bed
And feels like something, with the door ajar,
Crouched in the bracken, alert, with big eyes
For the hunter, death, disaster.

PETER REDGROVE

Stillbirth

Labour was normal, a birth, like any other.
But long, for bearing nothing but a stone;
Pushing a stone of pain uphill for hours
Gasping for breath.
Hope did not die till later.
I had been heavy, a stagnant pool, no stir
No beat of heart, hands. Then
This cataclysm that seemed to presage life.
But, at the end, no cry.

Under the half-death of the chloroform
I heard the nurse laugh, joking with the doctor,
Thinking I could not hear. I knew, then
And a weak rage rose in my throat
That it was mine they looked at and held light.
I would have snatched it from them
Carried it in my mouth to my lair
With animal groans, and licked it back to life.

They took it from me, told me, all's for the best
And shut it in a box. What else to do
With something, not quite rubbish?
They did it decently,
Washed the cold face with colder drops of pity,
Baptised it for luck,
And put it in the earth where it belonged.

I never saw the features I had made,
The hands I had felt groping
For the life I tried to give, and could not.
But still, I sometimes dream I hear it crying
Lost somewhere and unfed,
Shut in a cupboard, or lying in the snow,
And I search the night, and call, as though to rescue
Part of myself, from the grave of things undone.

BARBARA NOEL SCOTT

Morning Song

Love set you going like a fat gold watch.
The midwife slapped your footsoles, and your bald cry
Took its place among the elements.

Our voices echo, magnifying your arrival. New statue.
In a drafty museum, your nakedness
Shadows our safety. We stand round blankly as walls.

I'm no more your mother
Than the cloud that distils a mirror to reflect its own slow
Effacement at the wind's hand.

All night your moth-breath
Flickers among the flat pink roses. I wake to listen:
A far sea moves in my ear.

One cry, and I stumble from bed, cow-heavy and floral
In my Victorian nightgown.
Your mouth opens clean as a cat's. The window square

Whitens and swallows its dull stars. And now you try
Your handful of notes;
The clear vowels rise like balloons.

SYLVIA PLATH

One poet's experience of parenthood

Bear-Hug

Childlessness crushed me,
a bear-hug

I never breathed
till I bore her

though now in her clasp
I hurt

being drawn so far
from my breathless life

Why compose
on a guitar
at six years old
a curious refrain
entitled
Horse Mane?

But she does

PENELOPE SHUTTLE

Miss Butterfly, Miss Moth

Butterfly and moth,
one primrose pale,
the second grey as god himself,
both dead,
the child keeps them
in a Flora carton
with air-holes pierced in it;
airy tomb,
plastic sepulchre
she has given to moth and butterfly
 as a sanctuary
where they can find peace,
transform to their next stage
which, she sings hopefully,
(Miss Butterfly, Miss Moth),
will be fairy or elf
but fears will be only wing-tip dust,
a tick of mist;

for the child has undreamed her song before.

PENELOPE SHUTTLE

Masks

The child has masks
It is easy to forget this.
Behind her masks
of today and tomorrow
is yesterday's face,
see, she is still too young
to understand anything
but food and sleep.
My threats are no way
to break her silences,
to curb her fires,
there must be a way
of speaking
that runs true and clear
from the womb's infant
to the child who faces the world,
her school masks of fear and pride
sprouting fresh each day;
she flinches but does not retreat;
she wears a bruised lazy-mask,
a stiff oldfashioned anger-mask,
one summer mask glitters, gifted with speech,
another is a poke-tongue laughter mask.
She has her heroic silver bedtime mask.
My own pedantic mother-mask watches.

There must be a language
for me to speak, for her to utter;
a language where the sweet and the bitter
meet; and our masks melt,
our faces peep out unhurt, quaint and partial as babies.

PENELOPE SHUTTLE

Chrysalis

Like all mothers
I gave birth to a beautiful child.
Like all mothers
I wiped myself out,
vanished from the scene
to be replaced by a calm practical robot,
who took my face,
used my bones and blood
as the framework
over which to secure
her carapace of steel, silicon and plastic.
I was locked out of her clean carpentry
and smoothly-reprimanding metal.

Yet that robot's rude heart
flowed with love's essential fuel
because my child was one of the millions
of beautiful children
and knew how to tackle the machine.
She embraced the robot woman lovingly
each day
until her circuits and plastics wore away.
Now the soft real skin can grow,
the blood and breath move again,
the android is banished.

I emerge from the chrysalis
and go forward with my child
into the warm waters of the sea
in which we are both born at last,
laughing, undamaged
bathing alive in this salty blue,
my motherhood born out of her,
her woman's name and noon out of me.

PENELOPE SHUTTLE

Loving

Meeting

Meeting, 1944

(L.S. and M.S.)

I opened the front door and stood
lost in admiration of
a girl holding a paper box,
and that is how I fell in love.

I've come, she said, *to bring you this,*
some work from the photographer–
or rather it's for a Miss D . . .
Would you pass it on to her?

She's my sister, but she's out.
You must wait for her inside.
I'm expecting her right now.
Come in. I held the front door wide.

We talked a little of the war,
of what I did and what she earned;
a few minutes it was, no more,
before my sister had returned.

You're going? Well, I'm off out too.
And so we rose from our two chairs.
I'll be back shortly, Lily dear.
Shall I see you down the stairs?

That's all there is. We met again
until they took the Jews away.
I won't be long. I'll see you soon.
Write often. What else could we say?

I think they were such simple times
we died among simplicities,
and all that chaos seemed to prove
was what a simple world it is

that lets in someone at the door
and sees a pair of lives go down
high hollow stairs into the rain
that's falling gently on the town.

GEORGE SZIRTES

Nessa

I met her on the First of August
In the Shangri-La hotel,
She took me by the index finger
And dropped me in her well.
And that was a whirlpool, that was a whirlpool;
And I very nearly drowned.

Take off your pants, she said to me,
And I very nearly didn't;
Would you care to swim, she said to me,
And I hopped into the Irish sea.
And that was a whirlpool, that was a whirlpool,
And I very nearly drowned.

On the way back I fell in the field
And she fell down beside me.
I'd have laid in the grass with her all my life
With Nessa:
She was a whirlpool, she was a whirlpool,
And I very nearly drowned.

Oh Nessa my dear, Nessa my dear,
Will you stay with me on the rocks?
Will you come for me into the Irish sea
And for me let your red hair down?
And then we will ride into Dublin city
In a taxi-cab wrapped-up in dust.
Oh you are a whirlpool, you are a whirlpool,
And I am very nearly drowned.

PAUL DURCAN

The Lion from Rio

Golden inclination
of the huge maned head
as it rests against my knee,
his massiveness like feathers against me
amid this Rio crowd
through which he came to me,
this lion, my lion,
my lion of lifelong light,
padding unnoticed through the carnival.
Now his beast head rests in my lap,
golden flood, I am laden with it.
Looking up at me with his gently puzzled gaze,
he says helplessly, but I am a man, a man!

My own child could have told me.
He was a man.
How could I not have seen it?
Listen again, he is drowsily moaning,
I am a man.

PENELOPE SHUTTLE

New Face

I have learned not to worry about love;
but to honor its coming
with all my heart.
To examine the dark mysteries
of the blood
with headless heed and
swirl,
to know the rush of feelings
swift and flowing
as water.
The source appears to be
some inexhaustible
spring
within our twin and triple
selves;
the new face I turn up
to you
no one else on earth
has ever
seen.

ALICE WALKER

Rapunzstiltskin

& just when our maiden had got
good & used to her isolation,
stopped daily expecting to be rescued,
had come to almost love her tower,
along comes This Prince
with absolutely
all the wrong answers.
Of course she had not been brought up to look for
originality or gingerbread
so at first she was quite undaunted
by his tendency to talk in strung-together cliché.
'Just hang on and we'll get you out of there'
he hollered like a fireman in some soap opera
when she confided her plight (the old
hag inside, etc., & how trapped she was):
well, it was corny but
he did look sort of gorgeous,
axe and all.
So there she was, humming & pulling
all the pins out of her chignon,
throwing him all the usual lifelines
till, soon, he was shimmying in & out
every other day as though
he owned the place, bringing her
the sex manuals & skeins of silk
from which she was meant, eventually,
to weave the means of her own escape.
'All very well & good,' she prompted.
'but when exactly?'
She gave him till
well past the bell on the timeclock.
She mouthed at him, hinted,
she was keener than a TV quizmaster
that he should get it right.
'I'll do everything in my power' he intoned, 'but
the impossible (she groaned) might
take a little longer.' He grinned.
She pulled her glasses off.

'All the better
to see you with my dear?' he hazarded.
She screamed, cut off her hair.
'Why, you're beautiful?' he guessed tentatively.
'No, No, No!' she
shrieked & stamped her foot so
hard it sank six cubits through the floorboards.
'I love you?' he came up with,
as finally she tore herself in two.

LIZ LOCHHEAD

Staying

Last Chance, Last Hope

She clung to him like a witch
To her broomstick, like
A soldier to his angel.
She fell into his arms
Like jumping from a burning ship—
Without hesitation—from
A plane spiralling down,
Every control frozen, locked.

She wound her arms around him
Like a woman whom the sea
Has rejected already
Two times, knowing the third
Would be fatal. But he
Will save her. A small smile
On her lips at the memory
Of the waves, the flames, the shock,
The turbulence; nausea
From the drinks and ointments
They applied to her body
Before that launching.
It seems so distant.

He will support her,
Carry her high and away—
Her saviour, source of delight,
Last chance, last hope,
Her instrument of power—
With nothing left to pay
For other miracles
Should this one fail.

RUTH FAINLIGHT

The Marriage

They will fit, she thinks,
but only if her backbone
cuts exactly into his rib cage,
and only if his knees
dock exactly under her knees
and all four
agree on a common angle.

All would be well
if only
they could face each other.

Even as it is
there are compensations
for having to meet
nose to neck
chest to scapula
groin to rump
when they sleep.

They look, at least,
as if they were going
in the same direction.

ANNE STEVENSON

Scaffolding

Masons, when they start upon a building,
Are careful to test out the scaffolding;

Make sure the planks won't slip at busy points,
Secure all ladders, tighten bolted joints.

And yet it all comes down when the job's done
Showing off walls of sure and solid stone.

So if, my dear, there sometimes seems to be
Old bridges breaking between you and me

Never fear. We may let the scaffolds fall
Confident that we have built our wall.

SEAMUS HEANEY

Friend

In the white morning
we cuddle in our warm
world, toes friendly
in a hoard of blankets,
thighs glossing each other,
bums amiable. Me, I am starved
as a sparrow
after the long cold,
while the snow drives at
tree-trunks,
whirls at my window-sashes,
so fine
it spins
in the cracks and corners
of my house.

Up here
we are in a high galleon
on the crust
of a vanished country.
The sky is iron
behind birds, the road
a track of ash, cracking with
salt, and a scrape and
bang of spades echoes against
the black blocks of streets.

This light
bleaches and blues
skin; our noses of frost
collide.

You are no bull
to dig and spoil, but still
I warn you, some paths
are closed, impassable.

Between my house and yours
lies a city of snowfields;
still I need your steady
heat to set against
the bitterness of winter.

ALISON FELL

Parting

Waterloo Station

We clung together an hour,
walked, talked
laughed in earnest;
above the river, the sky
lay wide open and blue as ice.

Back under the station roof
words became plain,
practical, and our tongues
(for Waterloo would part us)
soon tired of them and turned to touching.
A hundred stares
faded as we kissed, unless
it was we who were absent.

I am alone here now.
This is again the most public of places
and my mouth
the most private of parts.

ROSEMARY NORMAN

'Stop all the clocks, cut off the telephone'

Stop all the clocks, cut off the telephone,
Prevent the dog from barking with a juicy bone,
Silence the pianos and with muffled drum
Bring out the coffin, let the mourners come.

Let aeroplanes circle moaning overhead
Scribbling on the sky the message He Is Dead,
Put the crêpe bows round the white necks of the public
   doves,
Let the traffic policemen wear black cotton gloves.

He was my North, my South, my East and West,
My working week and my Sunday rest,
My noon, my midnight, my talk, my song;
I thought that love would last for ever: I was wrong.

The stars are not wanted now: put out every one;
Pack up the moon and dismantle the sun;
Pour away the ocean and sweep up the wood.
For nothing now can every come to any good.

W. H. AUDEN

We won't play nature to your culture

Nature and Culture

The Lesson

A tree enters and says with a bow:
  I am a tree.
A black tear falls from the sky and says:
  I am a bird.

Down a spider's web
  something like love
    comes near
      and says:
    I am silence.

But by the blackboard sprawls
  a national democratic
  horse in his waistcoat
  and repeats,
  pricking his ears on every side,
  repeats and repeats
    I am the engine of history
    and
    we all
    love
    progress
    and
    courage
    and
    the fighters' wrath.

Under the classroom door
trickles
a thin stream of blood.

For here begins
the massacre
of the innocents.

MIROSLAV HOLUB

(trans. I. Milner and G. Theiner)

The Projectionist's Nightmare

This is the projectionist's nightmare:
A bird finds its way into the cinema,
finds the beam, flies down it,
smashes into a screen depicting a garden,
a sunset and two people being nice to each other.
Real blood, real intestines, slither down
the likeness of a tree.
'This is no good,' screams the audience,
'This is not what we came to see.'

BRIAN PATTEN

On a Tree Fallen Across the Road

(To Hear Us Talk)

The tree the tempest with a crash of wood
Throws down in front of us is not to bar
Our passage to our journey's end for good,
But just to ask us who we think we are

Insisting always on our own way so.
She likes to halt us in our runner tracks,
And make us get down in a foot of snow
Debating what to do without an axe.

And yet she knows obstruction is in vain:
We will not be put off the final goal
We have it hidden in us to attain,
Not though we have to seize earth by the pole

And, tired of aimless circling in one place,
Steer straight off after something into space.

ROBERT FROST

Evolution

One wave
sucking the shingle
and three birds
in a white sky

one man
and one idea
two workmen
and a concrete mixer

one wave
shingle
white walls
bird and sky

two workmen
and a concrete mixer

white walls
wave and windows
lights and sky

five hundred men
and a computer

desks and days
white walls
lights and
one computer

rooms and men
lights
one computer
desks and days

rooms and windows
desks and lights
lights and days
and days and rooms
desks and rooms
days and lights
daylight in

dayrooms
and days
in desks
and days
in days

and one man
mad
dreaming of

one wave
sucking the shingle
and three birds
in a wide sky

EDWIN BROCK

Lore

Job Davies, eighty-five
Winters old, and still alive
After the slow poison
And treachery of the seasons.

Miserable? Kick my arse!
It needs more than the rain's hearse,
Wind-drawn, to pull me off
The great perch of my laugh.

What's living but courage?
Paunch full of hot porridge,
Nerves strengthened with tea,
Peat-black, dawn found me

Mowing where the grass grew,
Bearded with golden dew.
Rhythm of the long scythe
Kept this tall frame lithe.

What to do? Stay green.
Never mind the machine,
Whose fuel is human souls.
Live large, man, and dream small.

R. S. THOMAS

Heirloom

She gave me childhood's flowers,
Heather and wild thyme,
Eyebright and tormentil,
Lichen's mealy cup
Dry on wind-scored stone,
The corbies on the rock,
The rowan by the burn.

Sea-marvels a child beheld
Out in the fisherman's boat,
Fringed pulsing violet
Medusa, sea-gooseberries,
Starfish on the sea-floor,
Cowries and rainbow shells
From pools on a rocky shore.

Gave me her memories,
But kept her last treasure:
'When I was a lass', she said,
'Sitting among the heather,
'Suddenly I saw
'That all the moor was alive!
'I have told no-one before'.

That was my mother's tale.
Seventy years had gone
Since she saw the living skein
Of which the world is woven,
And having seen, knew all;
Through long indifferent years
Treasuring the priceless pearl.

KATHLEEN RAINE

The Day Mama Dot Takes Ill

The day Mama Dot takes ill
The continent has its first natural
Disaster: chickens fall dead on their backs
But keep on laying rotten eggs; ducks upturn
In ponds, their finned feet buoyed forever;
Lactating cows drown in their sour milk;
Mountain goats lose their footing on ledges
They used to skip along; crickets croak,
Frogs click in broad daylight; fruits drop
Green from trees; coconuts kill weary travellers
Who rest against their longing trunks;
Bees abondon their queens to red ants and bury
Their stings in every moving thing; and the sun
Sticks like the hands of a clock at noon,
Drying the very milk in coconuts to powder.

Mama Dot asks for a drink to quench her feverish
Thirst: it rains until the land is waist-deep
In water. She dreams of crops being lost:
The water drains in a day leaving them intact.
She throws open her window to a chorus and rumpus

Of animals and birds. . . and the people carnival
For a week. . . still unsteady on her feet
She hoes the grateful ashes from the grate
And piles the smiling logs on it.

FREDERICK D'AGUIAR

Small Questions Asked by the Fat Black Woman

Will the rains
cleanse the earth of shrapnel
and wasted shells

will the seas
toss up bright fish
in wave on wave of toxic shoal

will the waters
seep the shore

feeding slowly the greying
angry roots

will trees bear fruit

will I like Eve
be tempted once again
if I survive.

GRACE NICHOLS

UNIT
6

Witnesses

I, too, sing America

I, too, sing America.

I am the darker brother.
They send me to eat in the kitchen
When company comes,
But I laugh,
And eat well,
And grow strong.

Tomorrow,
I'll sit at the table
When company comes.
Nobody'll dare
Say to me,
'Eat in the kitchen',
Then.

Besides,
They'll see how beautiful I am
And be ashamed –

I, too, am America.

LANGSTON HUGHES

Still I Rise

You may write me down in history
With your bitter, twisted lies,
You may trod me in the very dirt
But still, like dust, I'll rise.

Does my sassiness upset you?
Why are you beset with gloom?
'Cause I walk like I've got oil wells
Pumping in my living room.

Just like moons and like suns,
With the certainty of tides,
Just like hopes springing high,
Still I'll rise.

Did you want to see me broken?
Bowed head and lowered eyes?
Shoulders falling down like teardrops,
Weakened by my soulful cries.

Does my haughtiness offend you?
Don't you take it awful hard
'Cause I laugh like I've got gold mines
Diggin' in my own back yard.

You may shoot me with your words,
You may cut me with your eyes,
You may kill me with your hatefulness,
But still, like air, I'll rise.

Does my sexiness upset you?
Does it come as a surprise
That I dance like I've got diamonds
At the meeting of my thighs?

Out of the huts of history's shame
I rise
Up from a past that's rooted in pain
I rise
I'm a black ocean, leaping and wide,
Welling and swelling I bear in the tide.

Leaving behind nights of terror and fear
I rise
Into a daybreak that's wondrously clear
I rise
Binging the gifts that my ancestors gave,
I am the dream and the hope of the slave.
I rise
I rise
I rise.

MAYA ANGELOU

Right on: white america

this country might have
been a pio
            neer land
once.
    but.   there ain't
no mo
        indians   blowing
custer's mind
                with a different
image of america.
                        this country
might have
            needed shoot/
outs/daily/
            once
                    but. there ain't
no mo real/white/   allamerican
                        bad/guys.
just.
    u & me.
            blk/and un/armed.
this country might have
been a pion
            eer land.   once.
                        and it still is.
check out
        the falling
gun/shells   on our blk/tomorrows.

                                    SONIA SANCHEZ

Las' Rights

Gunclick/
hopesfears
lovehate
the move
to make
this friday
comin on
strong a need
to see the John
or tell the baas
jus how the cash
real low
or where the
present alms
presented every
month should go:
bittahsulphah
acrid lifesmell
(or how the taste
of fresh white
bread upset
the bammi Negrah
yam an even
though the
price is high
the saltfish
low real low)
a new
suit a tery
lene for the
weddin next
week an Christ
masiscominthe
gooseisgettinfat
so please baas,
please put a
somethin
in your poor
bredda hat
/Gunflash/
done

BRIAN MEEKS

Yuh Hear Bout?

Yuh hear bout di people dem arres
Fi bun dung di Asian people dem house?
Yuh hear bout di policeman dem lock up
Fi beat up di black bwoy widout a cause?
Yuh hear bout di M.P. dem sack because im refuse fi help
im coloured constituents in a dem fight 'gainst deportation?
Yuj noh hear bout dem?
Me neida.

VALERIE BLOOM

Witnesses

We three in our dark decent clothes,
unlike ourselves, more like the three
witches, we say, crouched over the only
ashtray, smoke floating into our hair,

wait. An hour; another hour.
If you stand up and walk ten steps
to the glass doors you can see her there
in the witness box, a Joan of Arc,

straight, still, her neck slender,
her lips moving from time to time
in reply to voices we can't hear:
'I put it to you. . . I should like to suggest. . . '

It's her small child who is at stake.
His future hangs from these black-clad
proceedings, these ferretings under her sober
dress, under our skirts and dresses

to sniff out corruption: 'I put it to you
that in fact your husband. . . that my client. . .
that you yourself initiated the violence. . .
that your hysteria. . .' She sits like marble.

We pace the corridors, peep at the distance
from door to witness box (two steps up,
remember, be careful not to trip
when the time comes) and imagine them there,

the ones we can't see. A man in a wig
and black robes. Two other men
in lesser wigs and gowns. More men
in dark suits. We sit down together,

shake the smoke from our hair, pass round
more cigarettes (to be held carefully
so as not to smirch our own meek versions
of their clothing), and wait to be called.

FLEUR ADCOCK

Witch

They told me
I smile prettier with my mouth closed.
They said–
better cut your hair–
long, it's all frizzy,
looks Jewish.
They hushed me in restaurants
looking around them
while the mirrors above the table
jeered infinite reflections
of a raw, square face.
They questioned me
when I sang in the street.
They stood taller at tea
smoothly explaining
my eyes on the saucers,
trying to hide the hand grenade
in my pants pocket,
or crouched behind the piano
They mocked me with magazines
full of breasts and lace,
published their triumph
when the doctor's oldest son
married a nice sweet girl.
They told me tweed-suit stories
of various careers of ladies.
I woke up at night
afraid of dying.
They built screens and room dividers
to hide unsightly desire
sixteen years old
raw and hopeless
they buttoned me into dresses
covered with pink flowers.
They waited for me to finish
then continued the conversation.
I have been invisible,
weird and supernatural.

I want my black dress.
I want my hair
curling wild around me.
I want my broomstick
from the closet where I hid it.
Tonight I meet my sisters
in the graveyard.
Around midnight
if you stop at a red light
in the wet city traffic,
watch for us against the moon.
We are screaming,
we are flying,
laughing, and won't stop.

JEAN TEPPERMAN

Tell Me

So tell me what you have
to give: I have strong limbs
to make a lap of love
a brow to gaze at in
the quiet times half light and
lips for kissing: I'm well
fixed for all love's traffic

And further, I've an ear
open around the clock
you know, like those phone
numbers that you call at
anytime. And such soft eyes
that smile and ferret out
the truth. Extraordinary

eyes, and gentle – you can see
yourself. It's strong and warm
and dark, this womb I've got
and fertile: you can be
a child and play in
there: and if you fall and
hurt yourself it's easy

to be mended: I know
it sounds a little much
but that's the way it seems
to me. So tell me, brother

what have you to give?

PAMELA MORDECAI

Index